AF445229

A Travelers Legacy

By Gerald W. Alvis

Copyrights @ 2023

ALL RIGHTS RESERVED

No part of this book may be reproduced or transmitted in any form or by any means, electronic or mechanical, including photocopying, recording, or by any information storage and retrieval system without the written permission of the author, except were permitted by law

Table of Contents

About the Author

I have been married to my High School Sweetheart for 46 years. I'm the father of 2 sons and grandfather to 5. I enjoy traveling, writing, and playing guitar, and I am passionate about Italian sports cars (Maserati's) and off-roading.

I retired, following a career of 37 years as a CAT Scan Engineer. I co-authored and taught the curriculum for a new generation of engineers. I built a Clinical Engineering Dept from scratch at a Regional Medical Center. I worked with Japanese and Indian Engineers to develop and implement artificial Intelligence.

I Co-owned a company that wrote and taught Joint Commission Compliance to two corporations at 24 sites. I assisted two medical facilities in receiving their accreditation.

I'm a Navy Veteran; I serviced the radar and computers aboard the world's first super aircraft carrier, the USS Forrestal CV59.

I am a writer; my book "Gerald's Reverie" was published in Nov 2023. It's available on Amazon in all formats and is being marketed to the big box stores, including Barnes and Noble. My writings are published monthly in Old Huntsville. I have been published in sports magazines.

I am an Ironman Triathlete and an Ironman Certified Coach; I also coached Bodybuilding and participated in the Mr. Tennessee Contest.

I've owned a small LLC selling paintball equipment and supplies with my family. We have held tournaments throughout the US.

I have served as a Reserve Police Officer. We have participated in Therapeutic Foster Care.

I earned my License in Massage Therapy and Certification as a Neuro Muscular Therapist. I also filled in and taught one semester. I advised on the curriculum.

I hold 16 certifications with the Professional Association of Diving Instructors, including Assistant Instructor, Dive Master, and Gas Blender.

We are active at our local Church, and I serve as Secretary for our HOA.

Ann Alvis

Thank you for this Jour ney we have shared!

FOREMAN

Introduction

When I first began my relationship with this fascinating gentleman, I saw him as a comrade in arms, as Navy Sailors. In a very short time, I learned what an insightful, thoughtful, and intelligent man he is.

During our conversations, we discussed experiences and what we found rewarding. One of the most interesting topics that resonated the most with me was aging. It is not just about accepting the things we can no longer do or the lives we built with our blood, sweat, and tears; it was his appreciation of the things often ignored in the everyday rush.

It yielded a new understanding of my life and emphasized the need for and importance of being the spouse one could lean on and grow with while living one's best life. Now, at this age, he shared his discovery of art and the beauty of music, nature, paintings, operas, and plays. Or just the quietness of an afternoon sitting in his backyard enjoying a water fountain featuring a statue named "Katina." This is part of the payoff for the prior work, the recognition of the brevity of our time, and the awareness of a simpler life and its pleasures.

Gerald's writings are about what he sees and discovers every day. All the years before were his steppingstones to be able to do what he has always wanted to do. He is leaving a Legacy. A legacy that his family and friends will forever be able to enjoy in the form of words and observations. His way of viewing our world provides an upbeat, healthy, and beautiful way to savor the best of what we have when we take time to observe and appreciate.

Kristi Jones

Dedication

This book, its contents, observations, and the interlaced hopes and dreams are dedicated to those who come after me.

To my Grandchildren: Ryan, Courtney, Gabbie, Jacob (Roo), and Jerimiah. You are the greatest joy in my life. I pour all I can and am into you!

To my Sons and your wives, Wayne Greg, you are all that is best in me! Being a part of your life and watching you grow and take your place in the world has brought me much happiness and comfort. It's your turn now as the next generation builds. What a ride it has been! JC and Sam, you've taught me happiness, which I've never known, being a dad to girls, thanks for your love and patience. To Larry my Florida Clone.

To my son/nephew and his wife, whom I call daughter, Kenneth and Debbie, the world is a better place because you help protect and heal life. Tessa D and Bon Bon,... well, look out, world!!! I will fill the gap my brother left; I can and will be there.

To Ealy thank you for Samantha and your wisdom.

To Jeremey, Bretinie and Jacob, Ryder and Willa Kate

To Will, Madison, and three sparkplugs full of life, Anders, Ada, and Nora, you define adventure.

To Jerry and Janet Ramsey thank you for J.C.! A nod to Kendra and Alex and your children.

To Aunt Gayle one of the most giving and hard-working women I know!

To the biggest firecracker on the planet Bonnie Sachs, you continually amaze me!

And in Memory of Harold.

To Jake, Jud, and Ms. M, you will always be a part of my life. I've enjoyed the memories, and there is more to come. A nod to Kevin and Dallas, now Drew and Krista have joined in the adventures. And welcome Alea!

And to three girls rapidly becoming ladies, Nora, Emma, and Abigale, my life is richer because of you.

And you Horsie!

All the above has hinged on one person. Without her, this would not have ever been.

It was my best choice in life and though the first book was dedicated to you your presence and love are interwoven deeply in this one as well.

To my loving Wife Ann, Thank You!

Gerald W. Alvis

A Special Nod to my Publisher

At Old Huntsville Magazine

Thank you, Cathey!

It's when we sit in silence, that's when we discover where the noise resides!

Baseball, an Old Barn, and a Wedding

It's at the end of a full and beautiful day as I pen this article. It's been three decades since I've thrown pitches and assisted with batting on at Tball/minor league field and my 8-year-old Grandson smiled almost in disbelief when I shared that I was once his Daddy's coach. Getting a ground ball takes a lot of effort these days and the throwback to the pitcher told me how long it had been since I had played catch! I enjoyed it immensely but when we got back to my son's home in Tennessee I spoke with my wife about the feelings of relevancy. I know our Grandson hears our voices in the stands and occasionally looks for our faces so he can wave but those days of our youth and some abilities have long passed. We now yield to the following generations.

But no time to further ponder there was a wedding to attend this Saturday, so off we went. It was a beautiful ceremony in a beautiful venue, a renovated barn in the country. About halfway through the nuptials as I snapped a few photos and began to think of my wife, almost in queue she turned and flashed her beautiful smile. Almost a half-century ago, we said our vows and my... how we've changed. I scanned the barn again and realized it too was once something a lot different.

We've both evolved in our roles this oak structure and I. We celebrate time still standing and being filled with love.

Regatta

The girls had been noticing some small fish near the shore of our community pond. They remembered some small nets we acquired on vacation to capture the tiny crabs that scurried along the beach. So, with some stale bread, the nets, and high hopes, we were off on an adventure. At first unsuccessful, they soon mastered the scoop method, placing several quickly named small breams in a plastic bag. Other creatures that huddled close to shore were also noted, in the catch, tadpoles, crawfish, and some icky bugs.

The local raccoons enjoy a sort of oyster bar at different locations along the shoreline. They leave behind a cluster of shells that once contained the delicacy they enjoyed during prior evenings. When rinsed clean, the shells' colors span the spectrum with deep blues and hints of red.

It's here that I learned something. My youngest granddaughter launched one-half of these mussels on the pond stillwaters. Moreover, a brisk breeze began pushing it along. I had never thought of even trying that! I smiled as I watched it move further from its port. Then the wind gusted strongly; it picked up a dried, crunchy-looking sweetgum leaf, landing it not far from this makeshift shell boat. A race had begun, the leaf now leading but both nicely making way. It was clear it would be the winner when once again, another stronger breeze brought several more pieces of spent foliage to the event. Soon a regatta of a dozen or more "boats" were reaching for the other shore.

These items from nature seemed to have been at the end of their journey! There were no other apparent options for them. But look what happens when a little help is given. A little girl believed differently, and the wind sought out those whose sails were still lifted.

Viewpoints

I received an email yesterday from my oldest son, who is now in his early 40s. He was going through some old CDs and found two documents, both written 20 years ago. One was for a college project my son had written. The assignment was about the goals after college and why and he explored several options in his paper. Mine was retrospective, looking back as a man in my early forties. I wanted to leave a note about where I had been and what I had seen and accomplished so far in my journey. Some of the reminiscings were about the time I spent on board the ship and the places I used to visit. I wanted my children (and my readers) to know more than the figure but understand the man. We must do both for balance, the whole dream thing, and reflection, but that's for the pauses, the quiet moments of our mind's leisure time.

So much of life is missed pondering old mistakes pining for lost loves and moments or perhaps reliving old glories. Others dream of flight but aren't in the now long enough to build their wings. The resolution is never to allow what you can't change or control or interfere with enjoying and being where you are. It's okay to check your compass, and it's okay to read the ship's log; both guides are points of reference and help us steer. Both decisions made and enjoyments of life are best in the present time. We can reflect in the harbor… plotting our next course.

Wishing you fair winds and following seas!

southern
MARKETPLACE
BARN SALE

The Rain and Adventure

There is nothing much on the schedule for the rest of the day, just a few errands. My wife is

shopping, and I got the house to myself, so I got a little crazy. I turned up my guitar loud and played for a while. I cleaned off my desk and emptied the trash, but I had some alone time. I felt I should be more adventurous. I decided to leave the lid up, use the good scissors to open some boxes then run with them. I might even kick a few ice cubes under the fridge should they fall astray.

As carefree as this sounds, the quiet is almost deafening. I miss the sounds of mischievous laughter and the love felt by those close to me. I'm in a home that now feels like a cavern, creating a sort of sensory deprivation. But this doesn't last for long...

I looked outside to see that gentle rain, the first in a while, and ya, that's always soothing! I could hear the pattering increase against my window. I was watching the droplets race down the panes. Ahh, what a gentle beat the thunder was following!

Growth and repair come to the body in the solitude of sleep and, I believe to a certain extent, the mind via dreams. So instead of reaching for the new book I bought or watching any of the myriad of movies available these days, I will listen in silence and see what I can learn, and I wonder what clarity will form. It's in the calm that we become aware. That's where we adjust the rudder and define our own view of happiness. The honesty of self is found here, inventory is taken, and I believe the templates of our dreams are where we foretell our future.

And if we are going to cry out to the heavens, can I not sit still long enough and listen to the universe's whispered reply?

Two lovely and mysterious ladies in France

Willow

There is a willow that stretches into our yard! Its branches sway rhythmically with a crisp fall breeze. Several limbs are about a foot from the ground and bounce as if reaching for the earth.

I'm divided. Do they want to return to whence they came? Are they gracefully bowing to the sun? Is it a polite curtsy that this canopy is performing? I asked my wife she said they were dancing in the wind. I thought about it; yea, I prefer her view!

Visions of Fall

I'm seeing more reds now in the trees! There are some yellows and browns, but these crimson colors catch my eye!

These signs of the seasons come along with the crisp air and delayed mornings, but not to worry, chivalry is not dead!

Deciduous and conifer trees will soon provide a blanket to warm the ground from whence they came!

Fall Music

We have almost a complete spectrum of fall colors here in our neighborhood. It's beautiful to the eye and music to hear the tiny cymbals oscillate. Each leaf is driven to its own timing by its conductor, the breeze. This song of the season, however, will not be silenced with the impending change to winter. Even after the mightiest oaks lose their grip on the foliage, the pines still whisper their high notes, and the discarded canopy does crunch underfoot. But it's not only the conifer's time. The branches that once held the weight of the umbrella are now free to dance, and when the wind tests their strength, they too join in the melody. It's not foreboding but foretelling. They say rest now and shelter, find peace, and reflect on what was with a promise of what will be.

Confident Race

I looked around at the several hundred people who had gathered this morning at a cross-country event. We had arrived early, ready to support my oldest grandson in his efforts. Seems I was the oldest one attending. Then after the pistol was fired, wave after wave of young athletes hurried across the terrain at best speed. I got to noticing something and could anticipate it. There were, of course, those cheering loudly for the winners of each iteration, and these would subside some for the middle-of-the-pack track hopefuls, their efforts being saluted as well. But then came the stragglers, those struggling to finish. Many had that same look of determination as those who had bested their times by several minutes. Though fewer were standing by the guided path to the finish, the volume and passion in the spectators' voices were nearly equal. You see when you're older, you wonder if things are going to be okay. We, the matriarchs, and patriarchs, are concerned about whether we taught or did enough to ensure continuity.

These kids are going to have to solve problems that aren't even invented yet; today, I'm at peace with this! There were children who excelled and those who didn't give up. That combination of disciple and determination is what our world needs, and these children were already living it!

P.S. On the way back to the truck after the event, my 7-year-old grandson asked me Grandpa, who would win a race, you, a turtle, or a snail?? I couldn't help but laugh! I told him I could take the snail, but it would be close to the tortoise!! A sense of humor will help as well!!

From the Hills of Tennessee Goodnight!

My Message

My wife leaned over in Church last Sunday and whispered checkout the two young men in the pew a couple of rows up. I averted my gaze and attention from the singers but still didn't understand what she meant, what I said in a hushed tone! 70's hair is back, she clarified, and when I looked back at the teenagers, I realized she was right. It has an exaggerated length in the front, which is great for flipping it or taking your hand and bushing it back into place. I had noticed it on my 13-year-old grandson, and it seems the look is coming back around in a different decade and century!

When you are young, there is an inherent need to establish a difference from the ones before your time. It's seen in language, buzzwords, haircuts, and fashion. I won't say it too loud, but surely plaid polyester bell bottom pants have gone the way of the Dodo Bird. So here is a message to my grandchildren and those who never knew a time before smartphones.

Passion is a force best harnessed. Keep the fire in your heart but listen to wise counsel and the experience that comes with time; not everything has to be reinvented. Strive for high ideas. See the possibilities and augment others by seeing what's in them. What is held in mind is an indicator, if not a predictor, of the future. This belongs to you.

Your dignity can only be surrendered, never taken.

Let no one despise your youth or talents; many are bitter because they never used theirs.

Time is your asset; decide where, how, and with whom to spend it. Not one additional second can be created. While you are here, be a good steward so you can smile when you're old.

Be consistent but understand you will change your mind. Everything is temporary.

Technology has changed, but people, not so much!

Search for something bigger than yourself.

Hold someone else's hand; we weren't designed to walk alone but remember, we don't get to choose with whom we fall in love.

Forgive

Stay passionately curious, listen, feel, and observe; there is much to explore.

Find the courage to use your gifts!!

Reel Life

My wife is in holiday decorating mode. And with the help of our Granddaughters, our home changes with the seasons. The recessed glass shelves in the formal living room normally sport some of the different cameras I enjoyed over the years. These have now been replaced with flower displays and other festive items.

When I got my first SLR, I didn't think it could get any better! I could manually adjust my speed, and aperture, and gasp; it had an internal light meter!! I progressed over the years in my knowledge and cameras as technology and my budget grew. If you've ever been around one, you know what it sounds like, the buzzing sound of an autowinder located on the bottom of the frame. A new world then opened up to me with the purchase of a telephoto lens.

We were limited compared to today's machine gun mode of image acquisition. The film was expensive; the largest role was 36 frames. Though I did own a half-frame camera and a Polaroid, those are another story.

I like instant gratification as much as the next person, but there was something about the anticipation of seeing which photos "turned out" if you capture with the lens what your eye and heart saw. Gone are the small photo booths that sat in the parking lots of the big box stores. Film has gone the way of VCRs, CDs, and eight tracks.

Once upon a time, it was special to go into class, and there, set up in the back middle portion of the room, was a projector. It was a mechanical marvel that guaranteed the lights would soon be dimmed and we would spend the next 30 minutes entertained by the pictures stored on the giant reel.

I don't, however, miss the darkroom. If you've ever processed film, you can't forget the scent of developer and fixer. Everything is done by feel, and by the way, light is still faster than you if you open the door and fog the film bank.

Regardless of the media, photos allow us to revisit memories, to go back in time. We pause in the now and reflect. I believe it provides a grounding or centering in our lives. It's a perspective, a look at how far we have come when we ponder those fashions and hairdos.

My greatest lesson in photography came before my first shark dive. I had been experimenting with underwater photography, which is considerably more challenging. Before we went under, the dive master gave some advice that I still adhere to today. Take some pics but be in the moment; enjoy being here. I agree. I believe the most important photos are taken and stored with the heart and mind.

Fuzzy

Always receive a gift from a child with great enthusiasm. Their homework, clean room, or something they made may be all they have to offer, and they choose to share it with you!

This Picture is of Grandpa worm and his granddaughter. Gabbie brought these creations to me, and they reside in my office, so I will think of her throughout my day!

Near and Far

This is the constellation Orion. The three stars in the middle are the belt of the "hunter." About mid-way down, the sword attached to the belt is the Orion Nebula. It's not a star! It is gas and dust, a nursery for stars. It's the only Nebula that can be seen with the naked eye! The cool thing is though you and I are in different parts of the world tonight, we can both look up and see it at the same time!

There are 100 billion stars in the Milky Way. Approx 1 star in our Galaxy will burn out this year, but one more will ignite. We measure life in years, but with stars, millenniums seem short; they glow for billions of years! But, like us, they are born, and they die. It's a balanced circle of life on a grander scale, and we are not just observers; we are part of what we see!

I was a sailor, and the night sky on a darkened sea may seem a bit scary, but no, just the opposite it provides comfort, the familiar constellations. Betelgeuse is the 10th brightest star in the heavens to us. It's the top left-most star in Orion. You can determine both the position and direction from the stars. That's why we need to keep looking up!

Gerald

Internal War

A warrior must be willing to adapt and change to survive or he/she will not! Our greatest battles are internal. Regardless of the trial or contest, peace can only occur when our thoughts, actions, and beliefs align. It's not so much that you're willing to fight, you're willing to live for what you believe. That's the internal war, that's the most intense conflict. It will be the actions of those who believe not just the words that change the world. Share your life!

Eagles

But they that wait upon the Lord shall renew their strength; they shall mount up with wings as eagles; they shall run, and not be weary; and they shall walk, and not faint.

Isaiah 40:31

Santa's Helpers

I don't know of anyone in the military or veterans who consider themselves heroes; those terms are for those who risked more and gave...sometimes all they had. Still, when my neighbor spoke with us during our daily walk, I understood what she meant.

This past weekend, approximately 200 Veterans, first responders, teachers, physicians, and other clinical staff met outside Walmart and awaited the buses! They soon arrived to our applause, led by the enthusiastic cheers of a local high school cheerleading squad. One by one, with their guardians, they approached the entrance, and we were prepared for them with buggies at the ready!!

My wife and I had two young gentlemen under the age of 10; our job was to help them spend as close as we could to the 100.00 each provided by a local church! We kept tally as these Christmas gifts were added and then subtracted as new goodies were found around each aisle. To me, it doesn't matter how old you get; children's excitement and enthusiasm will always be contagious!! My heart swelled as their eyes grew; they had that look you've seen and experienced. It was a warm, gentle glow with a spark of adventure.

SWH, or Shopping with Hero's, was well organized and run. We returned our pendants/tags to the main tent as the boys climbed aboard the buses with wrapped packages ready for the tree.

Will they remember the toy in 40 years...perhaps, my face or name, probably not, but they will remember that someone helped, and they felt special and accepted. Why do this? Oh, it was an awesome feeling, but somewhere down the line, this will come full circle; they will reminisce as they themselves witness the light in the eyes of a child.

A Warrior

A warrior knows moments of great conflict not just with the enemy but within the man himself. Something he is born to do, yet the end result is not his desire. Still, though, remaining at the ready should the need arrive.

In those intense, heated moments, all the senses are focused on a singular outcome, turning a challenge into victory and then peace. There is a transient internal tranquility that washes over and through the man who stands his ground to protect what he loves.

Then the quiet moments where the soul weighs and ponders. Wounds turn to scars, reminders of the price of commitment and love.

Then it's time, as it comes for all, to let go, perhaps the greatest difficulty. Purpose fulfilled one step over to a place that will honor what he did while the other foot tarries for a moment. Hands reach to guide forward while those behind hold onto the shell but not the man—a glance back, then a lunge into the next.

Tears then smiles, not perpetual mourning but reflection and then appreciation. May the poets remember!

Then for those that remain, shout out in unison to the heavens; such a send-off is deserved. Not in anger or pain but in recognition of a life lived fully, and it seems only fair to let them know he is coming. It's not that a man has passed, but the warrior has risen.

The Cardinal

Should I remain still or step closer to take the picture?

Midway through our morning walk, around our neighborhood pond, my wife whispered what is that in those bushes over there? I didn't have to ask what or where it was obvious. There was a brilliantly colored cardinal perfectly contrasted against the grey of the brush supporting and surrounding him. I'd never seen a more vibrant red. With my iPhone at the ready, I crept forward. He, however, noted my progress and spun around so that his back was toward me, partially camouflaging himself. The browns and dull hues now blended in with what had previously made him stand out in the landscape. He flew a few feet away as we got closer and then left when a female cardinal (they are primarily brown) came by and got his attention.

Humans are also an interesting species, but we tend to overthink things. We want to stand out but also fit in and blend. Varying from the norm, where it is safer and more comfortable, can be challenging. We crave that acceptance that comes with a group and the security it can provide, but we sometimes harbor self-resentment for holding back when we know the potential inside of us. Standing out can bring accolades, but it also makes one vulnerable to criticism and dangers, both real and imagined.

So, can being this independent individual yet being a part of something greater be possible? Does one compromise the other? Can they coexist? If both can be achieved, then how?

We are accepted best when we are ourselves. (Actually, it's challenging, if not exhausting, being anything else.) When we acquire our own approval for a worthy goal, our actions and beliefs align. It then we are drawn toward it and others who hold similar values. It's the law of attraction; it's powerful, not just in us but in nature.

I hope to see them again, the colorful birds. Perhaps in the coming months, if I'm observant enough, I may notice a nest, as life will begin all over again. I'm glad he took the chance.

I missed the photo but captured a memory.

By Ryan Alvis

Whale Sharks

It is counterintuitive to jump out of a boat 29 miles from shore in mile-deep water. But just below the surface was a creature I wanted to visit for the first time. It is such a truth that pictures never do justice to the event or beauty you're trying to capture. I've seen photos and videos, but from the moment we first located their pod, I knew I was in for a treat. The captain gives the signal and drops you off 50 yards or so in front of the world's largest fish. This title belongs to an aquatic giant known as the whale shark. The adults get about the size of a school bus, and the clear waters of the Gulf of Mexico provided me with the clarity to view the full length of this goliath swimming right for me.

So, a few yards away, the Shark decides to open his mouth. This is how they feed, scoping up krill and plankton along the way. Well, I know I'm not on the menu, but the void opening up could have easily swallowed me. All I could think of was that I was going to be on the news. I will be the only person that has ever been eaten by one of these.

Three beautiful moments occurred once I saw I would not become a modern-day Jonah. I can't say he made eye contact, but he looked right at me and moved ever so slightly to his left, avoiding the now imminent collision. We were close enough that I put out my hand and ran it down his back as he swam by. He then made the slightest flexion of his tail, pushing past me. The sheer power that propelled him forward with just a hint of effort was incredible. I remember looking straight down and then thinking of the depth below me. It's a bit unnerving to be suspended over a watery abyss, wondering what else could be there. I found comfort in surfacing and locating my ride back to the island of Isla Majeures.

I would perish quickly if left in this alien environment. But I felt, at least for a few moments, part of their world. I had no titles there or resources other than what I carried. That didn't seem to matter to the whale. We were just two creatures that came together at a place in time.

Printed Word

This morning I responded to a young lady who was so excited that she was being published in a magazine. It's amazing how words can sometimes jump off the page at you, and they captured her mood precisely! I couldn't help but smile, as I'm sure many did as they echoed similar sentiments to this fledging writer!

Seeing your words in print is an incredible feeling! A certain amount of validation occurs when it's deemed worthy by a professional and shared with others outside our usual circle of family and friends. It never gets old, and yes, you skip over everything else to see your name attached to an article that's gone out to thousands...or perhaps even more! People you will never meet on the other side of the globe can read your thoughts and opinions. You can enrich another life and maybe your own by sharing, knowing this will still be there for generations to come. It's a footprint, if you will, a wrinkle you've added in time.

This next paragraph would be different if my wife hadn't stopped by my office and said hello. I had it figured out and was ready to close this article, but with her appearance, a new twist was unlocked.

Every great love song or story is inspired by an extraordinary emotion bursting at the seams. And to those who can articulate it can strike similar feelings in the reader. While I love accolades, it's not so much the author or scribe. We are just sharing, making others aware, and perhaps helping someone else become cognitive of what's already there. It's the event, idea, or person who inspires the writer that's what should be celebrated. We, well, those of us who choose to wield a pen, are the conduit.

We each have a story! Share the beauty that is life. Let the world know you were here.

Super Girl

Grandpas teach, but we also learn a lot. We have time to ponder and pass this knowledge along less hurriedly. Walks are an excellent time for sharing. Jupiter and Saturn were putting on a brilliant show last evening, courting the moon as they passed across the sky. Whatever comes up, we talk about it as we stroll. But there are many pauses, for there is much to investigate at a pond. It's another step in their preparation for whatever comes up in the heavens and on earth later in life. So, do they get it? Does it all roll off and become forgotten? They may not remember the myriad of tidbits I include, but they do understand they are cared for deeply. Children emulate; that's how they learn; it's a form of practice for life.

Recently we had the spring on our double garage door break. Per the Technician, it typically snaps at the bottom of the movement. This is when the spring is loaded most, as it assists the motor in lifting. We have cautioned the Grandkids to wait until the door is all the way up before crossing underneath as a just-in-case preventive measure. Well, last night, Grandpa wasn't following the rules after our evening walk. My eldest granddaughter, who is 12, jumped in front of me and then threw her arm up over my head to protect me in case it all came crashing down. She didn't think she reacted, and I obligingly backed up while she still stood between me and potential danger. She didn't even look at the door; her eyes remained locked on me.

She had learned that there was something greater than herself, and she was willing to defend what she cared about without hesitation.

My precious God, can a man feel and be more loved?

Spark

The spark of life, chemically, genetically, and spiritually, however viewed, is a new energy that comes to be. Likened to a candle, the joining of wick and flame produces a light all its own. An existence begins where darkness and emptiness once thrived, now pushed back, fueled by an incredible potential.

Consciousness is formed out of atoms that can contemplate their own existence. It's a dynamic being that is never the same from the first moment till its elements are returned to the earth—a process or journey each of us traverses. Subtle differences are granted to spice up and augment an already incredible experience, yet we are more alike than different; we each search for meaning and purpose.

Driven by physics, yes, and it to its laws, we must answer, but other discernable yet unmeasurable forces act within and upon us. There is a sense of more than self, expressed as kindness, a subset of love, that can bring the embers of another wick back to life. Though counterintuitive, one's flame doesn't diminish from awakening another.

It's amazing this whole light thing. With our eyes shut, it can still be located; we are drawn toward its warmth.

We scan the heavens and ponder quietly our own inner space. We read to glean the thoughts of others. We are born curious about where we've come from, where we are going, and why we are here.

It speaks to me of more than a life of existence but of one filled with meaning, being more than we can now see.

Racing Rain

My breakfast was interrupted this morning by a tropical shower. The drops pattered with a tapping barely audible as each would press against the window. They would hesitate momentarily and then continue downward on their journey. Their presence and this climate are why the area is so lush and green, a real treat for the eyes.

And here is where I stopped…backspaced over a couple of paragraphs and left it alone. Creativity serves when it's ready and to my chagrin, I had wandered into the verbose.

Then later there was something that inspiration and creativity didn't take into account. It wasn't the basking of crocodiles on the banks of the iguana resting in the trees, it was a revelation, simplistic poetic words that like the photos I will carry home with me. There on the panel where the Captain would steer this small vessel were the words, "Live a great story"!

Reciprocity

I got the phone call today; a beloved long-time mentor has passed! She was my teacher and as much a magical human being as I've ever known. She taught me and everyone else with great enthusiasm, and she had a way of making you feel special. Over the years, we stayed in touch, I got to know their grandchildren, and eventually, they got to know about mine! We visited, as did they. Their cards and presents were always a welcome surprise.

Like many of you, I come from humble means, but that didn't seem to matter to her; she helped me believe in and develop the talent I couldn't myself quite see!

It became more difficult for her to travel, and she began to slip away. One of the last things she spoke of me through her husband was to ask if she could list me as a son in her obituary. Here was my hero asking this honor of me. There are only a few times where I've just lost it, but this touched me deeply. My tears were composed of myriad emotions, each waiting for their turn in my heart to speak. Her belief in me has done so much; my life has been better from having known her. But old thick-headed me, I didn't fully grasp the effect I had on her all those years!

Love is the original law of reciprocity!

Rest, Joan, but you do live on in me!

Ladders

Whether you are climbing out of hell or the ladder of success, the process is the same, and they can be both at once.

The initial step or decision to change is the hardest. Familiarity and confidence in that progress fuels the second effort, and new beliefs are born and affirmed. Something occurs with each new rung that is indelible and irreversible. From this unique vantage point, the world and how we see ourselves are viewed from a different perspective and light. We can see further, and our scope broadens.

These new heights are not limited and are determined by the decision to leave the security of both feet being planted. Then hoisting ourselves upward, we continue to move away from what was to what will be.

But don't hurry! Learn the lessons and tarry at each step. This knowledge and these skills will again be called upon in your journey. Learn what you are to learn where you are while you are there, then prepare, move up and forward.

This all begins quietly enough, a whisper that becomes a rhythmic mantra. It starts with a desire to change and see beyond self and these two words; can and will!

Southern Gentlemen

It caught me off guard, and I still ponder the remark, "You are the last of the Southern Gentlemen." I got out an awkward Thank You and a smile, but even after 30 years, I still ponder the comment.

It doesn't matter how "modern" we get; politeness and manners will never go out of style. I get being assertive, but we can better serve by showing respect and honoring others.

Be a guest wherever you go, especially in a different culture or country. My wife still tells the story of us at a restaurant on an Island that is a French territory. I quietly pointed at what I wanted on the menu, avoiding the mixture of my accent and lack of pronunciation. He said Oui Monsieur, and I replied Gracious...yea, International Man of Mystery. The waiter never missed a beat and went right on with serving us. As awkward as it feels, people do know when you're trying (I won't get into the chopstick incident in Japan). Read up a little on the customs, appropriate gifting, and phrases, and enjoy your adventures!

The word etiquette is a French word loosely interpreted as "label." There are ceremonial codes, proprieties of rank, events, and occasions that need to be observed in polite society. (Gleaned from Wikipedia)

Offer your seat to the elderly; for goodness sake, open the door for each other. Try it, smile, say, Sir and Ma'am. We don't know what others are going through, and courtesy may take a little of that edge off the recipient. Look people in the eye, shake their hands, and introduce yourself. These things cost so little but can make a difference in both your days.

Decorum is essential, which reminds me it's time to dust off my dancing shoes. I have my 4th Daddy-Daughter (Grandpa) Dance to prepare for in a few weeks!

Success

Recently at our home, a young man inquired of me concerning success. He was genuinely interested in improving, not just a secret or quick fix. I decided to share those thoughts here and was constantly backspacing. It sounded like another "How to Book." My challenge became to sum it up in a sentence—something bite-size, as concise as possible but with substance. I believe in developing the self we know deep inside is there, but the how can be daunting. So, for your Tuesday Morning contemplation, here you go. Also, please share your thoughts!

Master the basics and delayed gratification, yield to creativity, and remember you are constantly being interviewed.

Last Date

Writing has always been easy for me. It just comes out, but in other areas of my life, learning a skill is much more of a challenge. Drawing is my latest, and it could be prettier, but I enjoy it as it requires studying a shape or scene. It's seeing things again for the first time and then translating from the mind's eye to the canvas. Approaching three years now, I have been working towards learning the guitar. I'm still taking lessons from one the best teachers I've ever experienced, and I'm practicing with the music director at our Church and now with the entire worship team.

My younger sister, who comes up to visit several times a year, has been recording me, and let's say I've made progress when I review the early attempts. I'm sure I'll feel the same way next year.

There is an instrumental song by Floyd Cramer; some of you are old enough to remember. Skeeter Davis would later sing her version. It's called "Last Date." It's a sad teenage breakup song from 1960.

So why all the backstories? My three older sisters were gifted academically and musically. On a piano, one of those uprights that still had ivory keys, they would play this song in our home. They even took the time to show me the introduction on the keyboard. I can still remember a little of it. Last summer, my youngest sister forwarded me playing this tune to our remaining two sisters. A few weeks later, one passed, and two days later, the other is now facing severe challenges.

But I played for them!! I gave back a little bit to them and believe, as always, they were proud of their little brother. In the future, when the time comes, to get on stage, won't I be nervous?? No, not at all. I hope others enjoy my efforts; I'm playing for the same reasons; I will do my best and share the gifts I have with love.

Stuffed Sentinels

I first started to pay attention to it about four years ago. I was at a business office in Hino, Japan. I noticed that at various times during the day, people would be asleep at their desks. A definite no-no in the business culture of the states, I saw it with enough frequency I finally inquired about the practice. The broken English reply was when they are tired, they rest.

It was once a borderline guilty pleasure. Something allowed maybe once a week because, well, life is busy. I began to understand how to use it to recharge, reset if you will, and then be and feel better. My nap lasts about an hour and six minutes; the interesting thing is it's almost similar each time. No alarm, just an internal clock; it may seem a novel concept, but rest when you're tired. I've learned there is a reason it is a part of other cultures.

Acting on this knowledge and experience (it's easier when you're retired), I do just that, and life is better for me. I enjoy feeling rested. But it also yields some other unexpected benefits.

Recently I was at my son's home on a Sunday afternoon. Now part of my routine, I just let everyone know and slip away. My eldest had me lie down in my youngest granddaughter's bedroom. I use a fan for background noise, and I like the way it feels, but just about the time I was drifting off, I felt something being placed beside me. I opened my eyes and was staring point-blank at a stuffed fox and bear. My granddaughter had shared her favorite "stuffies" to comfort me while I rested. I grabbed one of them and held it close and listened to the stifled giggles.

It may be approaching the metaphysical, but some of you out there will get it. Even with your eyes closed, you can tell when someone comes in and checks on you. Perhaps it was a dream or wishful thinking, but she came back more than once.

Later I thought of the stark contrast, the image in my family's minds that walked by, but I didn't care. I had my two stuffed sentinels and an 8-year-old little girl watching over me, and I rested well!

Listen without hearing!

People say I love you all the time, and it's often without words.

Silent Color

I anticipate these moments each year; I saw the first buds on the trees two weeks ago. This seasonal event starts an eruption of Color, a yearly display of renewal. It's a competition between the yellows of the butter cups and the green pushing through the grey of last year's yard; so much vibrance is vying for my attention. Even the birds seem stimulated as they scurry around, and the doves have begun to coo. The warm and longer days now give us more opportunities to enjoy this new scenery, the painting of nature in the process. I find solace in this coming out of a season of rest. It's time to start anew with all the possibilities that it brings. All these hues in their hush signal its time.

Color is silent but not to the eyes; through that gateway, it speaks welcome, not to what has been but what will be. I find comfort in this.

"To everything, there is a season and a time to every purpose under the heaven."

Numbers and Time

An American President must be 35 or older, but there is no cap on the age requirement to date. So, with two potential candidates at 76 and 80, the age-old question gets emphasized. How old is too old? Is it across the board, and if so, should it apply to other key decision-making positions such as Supreme Court Justices and Military (Joint Chiefs) Commanders?

Recently a potential female candidate was labeled past her prime in her early fifties. Pilots must retire regardless of health or experience once they cross a certain chronological threshold. Being of sound mind should be a requirement, but who determines the standard, and then who decides?

Where do we draw the line if there is one?

The American people should decide concerning the capacity and abilities of our leaders! To have life experiences and finely honed skills negated by a calendar or some preconceived limit of human potential would be a tragedy and a waste of our most precious resource, life. Regardless of all the labels often applied to divide us, let us not let the grey in the hair (or lack thereof) be our measuring stick. Let it be the performance and potential of that individual. If you have the strength and drive to make it to the plate, pick up the bat in front of millions of people, and take the pitch, it is then we should decide if we want you leading the team. And those booing from the stands will always be there, never mustering but secretly admiring the courage of someone who hit it out of the park or at least gave it their best shot!

If we share opinions as a form of discussion leading to resolutions, then it's not a battle or matter of who is right or wrong; it becomes what is the best solution? Let's explore the options, even passionately so, and make the best decision with our current information and experience. We each can listen more; I've never seen the world from your viewpoint; let us find a better way.

Sissy 4

Heavenly Show

Gerald Alvis

The Poet of Greenlawn

Last night we completed our second walk of the day. The red hues of another sunset greeted us. Looking over my left shoulder on the opposite horizon, I saw the moon beginning its journey, ensuring the light we needed on the trip back from around the pond. In between, these stellar performers were another light show as old as time itself. Venus, Mars, Jupiter, and Uranus filled in the gaps between the Sun and our nearest neighbor. I am no different than those who gazed into heaven's millenniums ago seeing the same lights and asking the same questions. Orion will appear shortly, showing off its belt that the pyramids of Giza were aligned to in a bygone time. All of this is moving with greater precision than any Swiss watch. We are afforded a display each night, which will continue long after we are gone. Our lives are mere dots on an infinite timeline, and this is all a repetition of a cycle that is eons old. The gift we enjoy is the ability to contemplate and enjoy the vastness. And one day, we each have to give back the atoms we are currently borrowing, this shell that houses the consciousness.

If this life is all we have and nothing else beyond, then it's all the more reason to enjoy each moment; in our known universe, life is fleeting, precious, and rare. We are part of it and not just observers. We are in the play, a dance, and there is no such thing as a dress rehearsal. But if there is more beyond this life, it foreshadows the beauty we will understand in a different form—either way, we should pause to enjoy it as it is uniquely ours.

Thanks

Gerald

New Glory

I kept it stored and got it out every now and then. It meant a lot to me. My Congressman had it flown over our nation's capital. I even got one of those cool certificates stating the date and that it was done in my honor. Here's the background: she and I are pals who share a passion for triathlons. It was given to cross the finish line at the inaugural IRONMAN Chattanooga or IMCHOO. The year before, at Florida IMFL, my eldest son carried my father's flag, a veteran (Marine) of WWII, across the line ahead of me. It was a proud moment; it was also on my Dad's birthday.

The following year racing IMCHOO, I was on the verge of collapse one hundred thirty-three miles into the race. I can still show you the light pole I held onto to keep from falling over that night. What was painful was not just my body; pain is temporary; I know that quitting lasts forever, and holding that flag reminded me I fell short. So, I made a decision last night. To celebrate my Granddaughter's upcoming birthday, my wife and I joined her parents at school for lunch. I took the flag still in the original box, and she (my youngest granddaughter) and I presented it to the principal, himself a budding triathlete. I shared the story and my wishes. Old Glory needs to be waving in the breeze, not stuck in a box. I asked him to fly it over the elementary school.

It represents not just one citizen's success or failure, but a group of people united under one banner. It represents all that served to carry this flag, risking coming home under one. It is the symbol of freedom recognized around the world.

Yes, it had been hoisted on the building, itself the seat of power for our country, but to me, a better and more important use is for the kids to see it...and feel it in their hearts. It's their flag and their nation now. It's time for someone else to take it up and run with it!

Trees

The last rays of evening light highlighted the trees. Most of the reds were gone, but its branches and limbs were defined even at a distance. They were contrasted like one of those charcoal drawings you've seen. Boldly standing on display, patiently awaiting the modesty of foliage, these giants slipped into the night. I paused a little longer this last evening, capturing in my mind these arms that extend the earth's reach into the heavens. Though these conifers and deciduous examples looked nothing like the painting, I drew this morning.

Art is challenging for me. I've shown some of my work to my 12 y/o Granddaughter and then listened to her stifled giggles. Yea, it's that bad, but still, I enjoy doing it. I've decided to work on it. And then came the opportunity.

One of the greatest honors I have received is being a part of the steering committee for the VA. These projects help veterans to cope with stresses and reacclimate to civilian life. I helped pilot a writing program last fall, and when the art class was announced, I knew I wanted to be a part of it. It's one of the most rewarding things I've done listening to and encouraging those who gave much more than I did.

In my nonclinical view, these programs allow Veterans an outlet, a refocusing of thoughts, and a chance to see with new clarity. I looked at the trees as if I had seen them for the first time. There was so much detail there on the horizon. The painting was for me, and as we each displayed our art, I pointed out mine had that little hole in the trunk for the squirrel, but I had somehow forgotten my V birds in the background. I enjoyed hearing the somewhat embarrassed chuckles and encouragement. That's what it's about replacing some old emotions and memories with new ones. They are there, but it's not where we have to stay. In that sense, we have it better; we, unlike the trees, can move.

Challenged in Church!!

It's not often that this has happened, at least in recent years...but it did! It was just before the Church service began, and I had taken my usual seat. I heard a voice from behind challenging me; I turned, sporting my most serious look, and replied, "Accepted." Was it a doctrinal debate, politics, or about parking spaces?? No, it was arm wrestling. I propped up my elbow on my seat back, and so did he, and soon we were locked in mortal combat. I was holding my own until this seven-year-old pulled the "look over there" trick. Basking in his glory, I quickly readjusted my grip and went for round two, only once again to meet my demise. I would fare no better switching to thumb wrestling. He strolled away victorious. But it wasn't over yet!

The service had ended, and we were getting up and preparing to leave when a young lady broadsided me. It was an awesome bear hug, and I wasn't going anywhere. She announced they were having tacos today like they had shared with us a few weeks ago in our home. Once again, I had been immobilized. These young ones had put the elder in his place.

So, I'm sitting outside this evening, enjoying a cup of coffee, and collecting my thoughts. I looked down at the chalk artwork on the sidewalk leading up to the steps. I realized that this weekend had been a clean sweep. Yesterday I was also challenged by my 9-year-old Granddaughter. She said she could draw any animal I could name, and well, she did! The pathway to my home hosted a whole menagerie of critters.

If you've ever wondered why old people repeat themselves, well, sometimes it is memory. But mostly, we are trying to ensure we have downloaded everything we can to help you succeed; what we've learned, so perhaps your struggle won't be as great.

Pondering this, an amazing feeling has come over me. I'm overwhelmed knowing it's going to be okay!! These kids will solve problems that haven't even been invented yet. They are going where we cannot, but I can see it in their eyes. The uncertainty that we are sending them out to, well, they will overcome.

They are strong and will be ready, armed with courage, imagination, curiosity, and love.

I find peace and comfort in this.

We will always have Paris!

I believe my wife and women in general have a sixth, seventh, and even eighth sense. They have those eyes in the back of their heads, a built-in marriage manual, and they seem to know when we are up to something. It's hard to pull a prank on her, hide a present, or pull a fast one. Well, today, I reached a milestone.

We had a wonderful lunch today at my favorite restaurant in Nashville, then enjoyed a leisurely drive home. I missed our turn, but instead of turning around, I said why don't we take the long way and go through this small town with many antique stories. We can go shopping and see what they have! She was excited and immediately agreed! But I could tell her radar was up. I think I heard one of those beep-beep noises they make when she looked over at me! Anyway, we both claimed some treasures and continued our journey.

We took a break at McDonald's, pulled out of the parking lot, and there was a Burks outlet. My wife loves shopping at that store! I said, "Hey, want to continue our adventure there?"

At this point, she was excited but also concerned. I could tell she wanted to ask what had come over or what was wrong with me, but to her credit, she eagerly accepted. I thought the game was up; she was suspicious, but I threw her off the trail and said I'd wait in the car! That at least seemed logical to her.

So, I'm sitting here typing, wondering how far I can take this, but it's fun! I'm messing with her about messing with her.

But I must say she deserves the kindness and I enjoy the nostalgia of the antique shops! Gotta go. I need to google romantic cool things to say in French. I acquired a small print of the Eiffel Tower similar to another larger one in our home. You may have seen one like it as well. I call it the red umbrella. Oh, c'est si bon!!

Life is a journey best shared, with a little fun added along the way.

Forecast

Our descendants will look back at the 2020s in a hundred years with a smile. Our hairstyles and fashion will appear strange, and since it's viewed in the rearview mirror will indeed seem backward. And science, well, they will ponder how we survived without the marvels, methods, medicine, and conveniences of the 22nd century.

So, what is the best way from point A to B, from the here and now to this place and time I can only imagine and dream of?

The best path is not necessarily a straight line or even on the map yet. We listen to the esoteric; they are the future lookouts! They somehow see where and what we cannot. We give an audience to the historians, what worked before and what didn't. The visionaries have their role in the direction and how it must be accomplished. The task-minded apply all the wisdom and knowledge from above and create their masterpiece.

We must look for what is correct and best. The future for the coming generations is bright. I believe they will embrace a concert of minds instead of a contest of wills.

Consciousness

I enjoy it immensely when I have access to an expert. I do endorse reading as a way to reach inside the experiences and thoughts of another, but it adds another dimension in person. This direct form of sharing offers seeing versus supposing, tones versus italics, or punctuation. The pauses and inflections, the raising of the brow, the hint of a smile when the telling of a moment is relived. There is something in those eyes and micro-expressions that provides emphasis and clarity to the message.

I've had a chance to ask some deep questions from religious leaders, politicians, and physicists. They could have lost me in the jargon but instead, almost all the replies were simplified, I could tell they had dwelt on these issues for themselves.

I've had the opportunity to speak with three anesthesiologists over the years and each I asked the same question. "Where does the consciousness go when you put someone under"? One blew the query off, but two answered almost identically! "We don't know; it may be a spiritual thing!" Their lasting smiles spoke to me that they had contemplated this question perhaps with more curiosity and intensity than I!

In our brains how many neurons have to fire to create this cloud of self-awareness? At what point do chemicals moving around in grey matter think for themselves? Is this the mind, the soul? It intertwines neurochemistry, philosophy, and religion, this ability to think and contemplate this mystery. Is it individualistic, or are we all part of an oversoul or universal intelligence? Are we just seeds of life that one day continue on in another form? Have we always been alive, but that essence not recognized? Do we fade, and is this all there is?

There is more! Physics is an exact science of reproducible results. The formula's simplicity brings into our grasp mathematical verbiage as to why. They are as beautiful as they are revealing. Still, there is a calling, a universal need to scan the heavens that can't be put into formulas. There is more to know about outer and inner space.

It is a force that is real but can't be measured. It makes no sense at times, yet it means everything. Whatever our existence is and for however long, we are willing to sacrifice it for this one thing. It's the most tangible intangible thing we, as humans, can know. It is the variable of the universe amongst the vastness of constants offered. It is our motivation and essence, the power found in love!

The Physics of Harmony

Recently, I stumbled on a song from the 70s. Its best-known version was covered by a group called Gallery. Written by Mac Davis, it still causes my foot to tap and my heart to smile. The song is "I Believe in Music."

Music can induce a number of feelings in the listener. A great jam with the windows down can be a pick-me-up; there is always the blues, the spiritual music that can make our hearts soar, and a myriad of other genres and styles depending on our needs and moods. For those of us who remember, the late '60s and early '70s were a turbulent time. Assassinations had occurred; we were still at war in Vietnam; the civil and women's rights movements were still in their infancy. Watergate was also knocking on our door.

Well, I kept scrolling down memory lane and found another song that would likely fall in the bubble-gum pop category; it may sound cheesy to some, but to me, beginning to think about the draft and the world we were inheriting, it resonated. The video featured young people from around the world. The words still echoing to this author are, "I'd like to teach the world to sing in perfect harmony. "Yea, some of you remember!

So what does this flashback have to do with physics? Above my desk is a giant painting I won at an auction of Nikola Tesla. My favorite quote from him is, "If you want to understand the universe think in terms of energy, frequency, and vibration." Physicist Michio Kaku further captures and carries this in string theory, strings that vibrate rather than point-like particles. The ancient texts also hint at harmony "They were all in one accord." And I must mention the Beach Boys proliferating "Good Vibrations."

I've just finished German Theoretical Physicist, Sabine Hossenfelder's latest book, Existential Physics. Though she wrote it more for us laypeople, it is, at least for me, some deep stuff that I will review many times to grasp further. But I love how she ended the book! "So, yes, we are bags of atoms crawling around on a pale blue do in the outer spiral arm of a remarkably unremarkable galaxy. And yet we are so much more than this!"

We are each unique; the vibration or tones of our talents are sounded each day. Some softer, some sustained, but each note is needed to complete our opus! Music is mathematics blended with emotion, and the words of Ludwig van Beethoven, "To play a wrong note is insignificant to play without passion is inexcusable."

Music says what words alone can't, it is its own language, and that's why it moves each of us; it is as natural to us as our existence and part of our essence. It is a commonality like the rhythm of our beating hearts.

Harmony is possible; it's inherent, an expression that brings and binds us together!

Spring to Life

I got some vitamin D today, enjoying the moderate weather and the season's first-yard work. I did the usual stuff but added a bird box alongside the fence near an apple tree. Next on my list was planting a cherry tree. Their blossoms rival the dogwood and redbud, signaling another sure sign of spring. After scouting its new location and digging in the prevalent red clay Alabama soil, the tree was in the ground, getting its first slow drink from the sprinkler head. I paused and admired the work. Adding those two things gave me a sense of renewal. I mused over the shelter both would offer and anticipated their enjoyment in the coming seasons.

I looked over at the birdhouse, and a small head of a wren emerged. The tiny fixture had been quickly inhabited, and as an update, as of this morning, a full nest is inside. Its new life "springing" forth, a cycle that has repeated itself impressively for millenniums. Indeed, it may be common, even predictable, but there may be something new under the sun after all! My appreciation and enjoyment of being a part of it all!

Now it's time for the second Cherry Tree to be planted!

Blackberry Winter

The term isn't used much anymore as it is dated, but to the boomers, we remember hearing our parents and grandparents speak of it.

A wall of flowers is between the two ponds of our neighborhood, near the walking trail. The tiny white blossoms will soon yield some delicious berries. They make a delicious pie and my favorite jam! With the cold snap this morning and the arrival of these petals, you can see how this post-season event got its name.

They are just thorns in the winter, but they provide cover for many critters that scurry about this small field. If you look close enough when the leaves return, small nests appear; these homes above ground are also found among the briars.

Perhaps the term Blackberry Winter and this writer are both a bit archaic, but I don't mind. When you get old, you have to slow down; it's not an option, but with that, another world opens up. You notice things that were once hurried past. There is a beauty and purpose revealed and discovered even amongst thistles. It's there for us if we choose to see it!

Broken Value

I enjoy auctions and have begun attending yard sales (yes, I wrote that out loud.) Sometimes, I bring back stuff I shouldn't and really don't need, but at other times, the item interests me regardless of functionality or necessity.

Last year I purchased four hammers from an estate sale. The owner had used each for decades; the wear and tear and repairs on these instruments of his trade were like art and a testament to the commitment to his craft. I gave away 3 to family members and kept one for myself. I could have bought a dozen new hammers for what I paid. But what I was holding had a history and had served a purpose.

Last week we attended a yard sale here locally in our neighborhood. It's nice to say hello and meet new people. I walked away from one with, of all things, a music box. While in the Navy and even later, I would find music boxes and send them home to my wife so we have a history of them, but this one was different. Though lovely, it had scuff markers, and the music mechanism didn't work. I decided to repair it and ordered a new "engine" so this cherished chest, once full of notes and treasure, would be functional once more.

Kintsugi is similar to the Japanese philosophy of wabi-sabi. An embracing of the flawed or imperfect. Japanese aesthetics values marks of wear from the use of an object. (extracted from Wikipedia). I repaired the small wooden chest this afternoon, and with the expectation building, I turned the key, wound it up, and lifted the lid. The notched drum lifted the mechanical fingers one by one, creating musical tones. I can't quite place the melody; I started to "Shazaam" it but stopped. I just wanted to listen, and so I did.

The odds aren't good, me keeping it and all with two Granddaughters and Daughters-in-law. But if they so choose to ask, I wouldn't mind so much, and actually, I would prefer it if they did. Someone they love took the time to repair what was broken; in a now disposable society, there has got to be a lesson in there somewhere!

Old Huntsville
HISTORY AND STORIES OF THE TENNESSEE VALLEY
06/23/2022 12:00:00
AM
Gerald Alvis
5**3**212*****

Clouds and Compasses

Gerald Alvis

The Poet of Greenlawn

It is simply one of the most beautiful days I can remember! Cool enough for long sleeves and inviting weather for yard work!

The wind is quite brisk, blowing last season's leaves and some lawn clippings across the yard. The birds flying into the wind appear to almost pause. The contrast of pale and white clouds against a brilliant canvas of blue paints a dynamic picture for my enjoyment; I admired many serendipitous shapes as I looked up and watched each frame pass; then I wondered how the clouds knew where to go.

They were definitely racing somewhere enough that their puffy shapes were now elongated, wisped, and feathered by the frantic pace. They had no compass flying around, but then I realized it was ground control that gave them directions; the trees were waving to gather their attention, and then their branches would stretch and lean, pointing in the direction that they should travel!

Still

Last week just after a brief morning rain shower, I went outside to get the mail. I stood on the porch and realized I hadn't put my shoes on yet, and I started to go back inside. I thought about it and said to myself nah; I rethought it and said why not? I looked left and then right, no one outside, to see a grown man skirting a perfectly good driveway to walk barefoot in wet grass. I gathered the mail but paused about halfway back; I audibly chuckled as I curled my toes into the damp lawn. I felt like a kid again.

I've pondered my reaction to the moist turf under my feet. And I've thought of other times when I just stopped to enjoy. The coral reefs of the Grand Caymans are the best I've ever seen. More color and life are consolidated there than in the rainforests of Central America. At first, I would swim around fervently, trying to take it all in, but I learned to stop and observe what would come gliding by or perhaps what was hiding in the coral just feet or even inches away. I was propelling myself past a lot of beauty under the sea.

Riding in a hot air balloon teaches this from the start. It's silent up there as you are moving with the wind. But that's not the way it seems! You feel paused, perched high above a landscape that is scooting past for your viewing. It feels stationary, but at these speeds, it allows taking in as much as possible, a little at a time.

Consider pausing, drinking in the air and scenery wherever you are on your journey; even the ancient texts speak of being "Still." Exploring the world with less hurry and haste as we speed toward a myriad of deadlines and goals; provides additional meaning and appreciation in our travels! Yes, you may have to dry your feet off before returning inside, but this keeps life from just slipping away.

And to you, my readers, I'm happy we've shared a moment in time; I'm glad we met on the way!

Vision

It's a strategy I've heard many also use; first, buy numerous pairs of reading glasses, then station them throughout the house and in different vehicles. The aforementioned is not intentionally done, but it's a kind of rotation. You put a pair down somewhere then during your search; you find another pair! One form of vision tends to decrease as we age, but another comes into sharp focus.

Along with the years comes experiences, and knowledge of what is important, granted, that time has gone, but the struggles of achieving and sometimes survival are similar. It plays out in each new generation.

If you've returned to a burning building to drag others out of the fire or saved a drowning swimmer, you understand that you will risk your life. If you have raised your right hand and taken an oath, and/or you've held a hand and kept a vow, then you realize a greater love for ideas and others. If you've survived illness, you are proof you can come out on the other side. If you've given life or watched silently as others have left this world you begin to comprehend both its beauty and brevity.

There is a certain clarity if you've looked at another soldier and seen beyond the different uniform.

If you've ever had someone pray with and over you, as you are being wheeled into surgery, all the hoopla vanishes; you don't care if they have a robe, a doctorate, or if they are barefoot. Suddenly, it's just two people reaching for God together. It's important to forgive as well as ask to be.

As we begin to see others as human beings beyond labels the latter's importance fades. There is less of a desire to judge others.

Other joys fill in like that found in giving, including sharing homegrown tomatoes!

And even if you thought no one was looking all the times you got knocked down, they saw you get up! It is not that you failed, nor the task, however arduous or complex, they now know first-hand it's possible to recover and move on to where you are now, seasoned and tempered.

It's not so they can follow our path but create their own. Show them, show them the resiliency that got you through, that got you here! It's that resolve that gives them the vision and belief to flourish in a world yet to come.

Show them the best places to cross the river, where the best handholds are on the mountains, and teach them to navigate the sea! Let down a rope from the treehouse now that you're up there!

They need this focus, that peace, for we once knew these doubts and fears of the unknown. You are that beacon of light that says this is the way, and yes, you can. These glimpses into your life become tools they will teach their children's children.

This part of us lives on in others.

Rest

Most reading this are driven! To excel, to achieve! I get it, but there is a certain peace found in saying I've done enough for today! And no matter if you checked off your entire to-do list today or if there are many things pending.....

I tell my Ironman Triathletes I coach, that there is no such thing as a bad workout! If you show up and give it your best that's all you can do! There is an ebb and flow we don't control but are a part of...

So, rest tonight, did you make someone smile today, did you help someone who really needed it, did you enjoy some quiet time alone or perhaps a dance when no one was looking? Today was your day and so is tomorrow. What has gotten you this far will keep you the rest of the way!!

So, rest!! Tonight's photo was taken last night, sorry didn't have time to post! Venus and the moon, their dance slightly shrouded by a few wisps of clouds. This has gone on long before we came here and will continue long after...enjoy the now!

Goodnight!

Gerald

LifeSavers

No not the Candy!

Technically Lifeguards, they are stationed throughout the swim of the world's ultimate endurance race called IRONMAN. They wait in kayaks, boats with blue lights, and jet skis, scanning a field of 2500+ athletes as they paddle, kick, and maneuver along a 2.4-mile buoy-marked course. They are a welcome sight regardless of weather or conditions, but they provide even greater comfort in choppy water and are viewed with every other breath.

Divemasters in the world of Scuba have a similar task, but it includes emergencies (or preventing them) not only on the surface but below the water as well. Dangerous sea life and depths, confined spaces, or just staying down too long or coming up too quickly can have severe consequences!

Spotting someone in distress is more challenging than it may seem. They often struggle quietly, saving their air and not screaming out. A diver can even freeze up, afraid to move; a panicked diver can spit out his regulator on the way to the surface. Due diligence is required.

This weekend we honor those Veterans who gave their all, in service to our country. It can also be a challenging time for those who made it back. I ask you also to be a lifeguard, a lifesaver; let's remember, but also let's be aware of those who still struggle. 20 a day is too many.

The VA has many new programs to help improve quality of life.

VA.gov
800-698-2411
Hours: 24/7

Veterans Crisis Line
988, Select 1
Hours: 24/7

You are Only Old Once!

Twice last year, yep, two different doctors used the "A" word and sternly too!

I was clarified by my doctor (they all call me Mr. Alvis now because I'm older than them) after minor surgery. He said I could do whatever I wanted. I guess I don't hide my facial expression very well; as he turned to leave the room, he stopped, came back, looked me right in the eye, and said whatever is age-appropriate! Wow, this guy is good! At my annual checkup, more of the same; you know it's coming when the Dr. pauses, takes his glasses off, and gives that sigh. You are 63, not 43 he replied to my comments. As we age, these things become more difficult.

Yes, I know they are right, but I believe we think we will be the exception to reading glass and making noises when we get out of a comfortable chair. Whoever has said, I still feel young inside has had that awkward moment in front of the mirror when, ahem, the image of a seasoned person is now reflected back.

We are fascinating species to study, we all want to live long lives, but no one wants to get old, but as far as I can tell, the two are joined. I used to be the person who helped someone with lumber at Home Depot or assisted in putting luggage in the overhead compartment. I offered up my seat, but now well, time has passed.

Sometimes, age doesn't reveal all the wisdom you need, and even with all your life experiences, there is still room to learn.

My Grandchildren now assist me with projects; if I need something, they are there. My wife is always there but my Sons and Daughters-in-law keep an eye on me too!! So yes, their help is needed and appreciated; I didn't want to acknowledge what was obvious; I guess I didn't want to seem less than the man of 20 years ago. But I had to see past my ego. My family does what they do out of love; I see that now, and that's something I can grow old with!

A Little Golf

Older guys (over 40) I know you are wondering, what makes you irresistible at the Putt Putt Golf course. Before you say black socks and sandals let me say it's time to hit the update button! It's not how you use your putter as a cane, nor the 2 power reading glasses…it's rocking the floppy hat!! Nothing says stability and I have no sense of fashion and need help with this highly functional accessory!!

Next week appropriate attire at the beach or just say no!

Influences

There were three profound influences in my early years. Each of these men spoke of something I wanted to explore. One of them told of a world nearby that has hardly been explored. His series ran for ten years through the mid-sixties and seventies, and I was glued to the black and white TV watching the undersea world of Jacques Cousteau. I dreamed of going to the ocean and seeing these wonders for myself, and in 1979 north of the coast of San Francisco, my wife and I received our certification. I would pick it up again when my Sons were old enough, and now I've begun to share it with my Grandchildren. It is all true, but like always, it's better in person, and hearing my Granddaughters squeal through her snorkel when she saw her first fish on the Bahamian coral reefs was priceless.

An honorable mention goes to Gene Roddenberry for his science fiction of the '60s. However, another man with a unique voice I can still hear had a passion for the "Cosmos"; his name was Carl Sagan. He could take the complex and put it within my grasp so that I could ponder, no, not at the same level, but the same things. If you mix the two, you get questions like, do you die each time you are "beamed" transported to the planet? I still point out constellations and stars to my grandchildren.

The other was not just an American fixture but a world Icon. He remained humble and faithful to his beliefs, and though well "versed," he had a talent for making you feel comfortable "just as I am." His name was Billy Graham.

So, what are the parallels between those generations ago and today? Yes, they were experts, well respected, and they were all passionate about their cause and beliefs. They took us with them, were they leaders, yes, but it was more like I was walking beside them.

They taught us, helped us believe, and they took us along with them on their journeys. They encouraged us to explore the depths of outer and inner space; however, we choose to define it.

In a universe of physics and mathematics, we are the variable to the equation, a consciousness that can ponder all these things!

Kitchen Physics

I make most of the messes at home, so it's not unfair to contribute to the cleaning. I load the dishwasher and will do a load of towels, but I am generally disallowed from washing any other thing that has fabric. I will sneak in a load of jeans every now and then, but I know my limitations, and we agree to pick our battles on that one.

I get clothes and stuff to the utility room (however, not sorted in one of the four hampers.) Kind of like leaving dishes around the kitchen near the sink and dishwasher. Being in the zone isn't what Ann has in mind. I thought close (on the floor) or on the counter was enough.

Evidently, with Dishwashers, there are things that go on the top shelf and the same for the bottom and even how they are spaced. So what I thought was a simple job has a rhyme and reason, so I try to be a good student. There is one thing that is a mystery, the need to wash the dish before it goes in the dishwasher. And there is a thing called "soaking the dishes" in the sink. I just feel like I'm drowning in breadcrumbs.

I do have my suspicions that she waits and then rearranges my disorder in this mandatory kitchen appliance. When I open it to put the dishes up, they are in different locations and all orderly. Or could it be something else? What was first a possible accusation got me thinking, and what was born was a new theory in Physics based on deterministic chaos and Schrodinger's Cat!

Test it yourself! First, scan the entire kitchen and scout out the rest of the house for stray dishes and utensils, but as soon as the door is closed on the dishwasher and the start button is pressed, that's when the magic happens!! Look up, and there on the counter, an unwashed glass will appear!! Will you stop the dishwasher and add the glass or not?!! It boggles the mind!

Next week's topic will be "The lost sock in the dryer hypothesis." Maybe one was added instead!! See neutrinos or ghost particles for more information (though I have not ruled out a time portal.)

Intuition

When it's quiet, really listen, give it a few minutes, take those deep breaths, then listen. When all the static is squelched, your heart tells you where you really want to be! Your thoughts, go there automatically! This is not some great revolutionary discovery because it's intuitive, and we each understand it.

The battles we face are within ourselves; it's seldom really external. The conflict is that we don't listen to and trust our intuition; we grow frustrated even if we make progress because it's not in the direction we know we need to go.

Most of our ailments are because our innermost thoughts and deeds don't align.

Roundabout

Articulation is sometimes difficult if you are a novice or still grooming a concept. Maybe it's just a dream you want to share; perhaps it's a heartfelt emotion impeded by shyness or the possible pain of rejection or conflict.

This is where loneliness is born; amid a sea of people and even friends, the frustration and desire to be understood battles the norm we must project to others. It's interesting the need is so strong for acceptance that we deny the person we are and wish to share to fit uncomfortably into a preconceived mold.

But there are people out there who bring out the best in others. They possess the capacity to listen to and in between words and actions. They may inquire more to help, but they never probe. Gradually the motif of the heart is revealed, its construction even aided by one who takes joy in the progress.

They are the rarest of individuals who wield the skills of a mentor or a lover; they are teachers; they are genuine friends.

It is discovery, the moment of clarity that they live for, when they see the light come on in your eyes. The heart opens, and a passion for living is released.

They have a presence and peace we are drawn to. Their catalyst is kindness, but first, they have to become comfortable within themselves. They've been where you are and have now returned as a guide.

Destiny is a choice, and with these thoughts to ponder and apply, be aware it will soon be your turn to facilitate, and that in and of itself brings joy, and a sense of completeness as it comes full circle!

Army Bears and Snacks

I had received a frowning brow from my Granddaughter when she informed me the snack levels in the pantry were dangerously low! This was remedied with a road trip to Redstone Arsenal and the commissary.

At the entrance to one side is a display, a solemn and cordoned-off area. I started to walk right by, I mean, I didn't want to spoil the festive mood of movie night. But I stopped myself as I was about to stroll past and said no! This needs to be a teaching moment.

They rarely hear me well up. Again, we were having fun, but I asked them to come over, and I began to explain the display of an empty chair, a set table, and the POW-MIA flag. It hurt me to explain the abbreviations. The loss for the individuals and the families was painful to share. I wanted to inform these little ones about the sacrifices and somber realities that exist in the world they will soon inherit.

I got to see, hold, and enjoy my Grandchildren. There aren't too many days I don't think about that. There is a price for freedom, and it again will be challenged. The branches of services are different, as are the people in the ranks. But each of us said an oath that amounts to a blank check. We are an amalgamation of human beings under a common flag who vow to protect what is precious to us so that it is ensured and passed on to each new generation.

The soldiers walking around look so young... and that's because they are. They are doing the work that protects those who came before and those whose time is yet to be!

Reflection

There are many songs and much philosophy about life passing you by. Time is linear (except if you add some heavy-duty gravity and/or acceleration), but it does feel like it speeds up as we age. We have a limited amount of it in this form then the atoms that have been ours for this brief moment return to the earth. So, between now and then, what if we got the most out of these moments by realizing they occur?

What I mean is each day, reasons to smile appear, they materialize, and whether we acknowledge them or not, they are fleeting. I've not found a way to go back and recapture what slipped by, but time well spent can be relived in memories. Knowing I've lived in the moment is a comfort as the cake begins to sag from all the illumination on top.

You get what you are looking for, which becomes your reality. So, yea, there are evil and negative things that come at us, I get that. But be observant; look closely; the good and beauty are there, vying for our attention.

We can also gain cognizance of a secret, and it's a powerful one. We each can be that positive event in the lives of others. We can leave someone with a smile, a good feeling, a new confidence, or perhaps hope. You can't put that in a bag, hang it on a wall, or place it in a vault, but it's priceless. In my belief system, this is the best use of and way to enjoy the time.

A good writer is also an avid reader, and an effective teacher must forever be a student. I was pondering these thoughts in my head on our morning walk when Ann paused near the pond. She pointed at the reflection of a mimosa tree in full bloom. I almost walked right by!

You can almost smell the flowers, can't you?

Pass Along

Decide what kind of day you are going to have today. I get it; there are some bumper car moments, and granted, some things we can't control. What we can decide is if one or two things or moments will cloud all the others.

It's all about what we choose to hang on to and what is carried forward. Make a game out of it. Genuinely smile when you say good morning; it changes the tone of your voice. Be polite, honor someone, and show respect. Yes, it can make you feel good, and that is reason enough, but watch how it affects them, and then you realize it's not a game.

Beyond our Work, Facebook and Church face some real battles, and during those times, we are hypersensitive to both the good and bad. What I'm sharing is that a nice remark or compliment is amplified many times to someone struggling, and some people are hanging on by a thread.

So, yea, someone flipped me off in traffic or didn't hold the elevator door when they saw me coming down the hall. I don't know what they are going through. It is my choice to pass that on and perpetuate the feeling, allowing it to live inside of me or tell it to get out and replace it with how I choose to live and feel. It's independent; you know the outside influences and what we allow in and are.

You decide this morning; you are in control!

Scintillation

Explore those idiosyncrasies that are uniquely yours! I get it; there is protocol and etiquette, and yes, there is a time and place for everything, but make time for that spark that's inside. Use your gifts and maybe even stand out a little, be yourself; it's exhausting otherwise.

Exploring our own depths is the next step in becoming who we are meant to be, and sharing those honed talents is our gift back to the world.

We are each part of a mosaic, a quilting or puzzle, a conglomerate of voices and ideas that come to life when shared.

Poets go write, artists, please paint, and to the visionaries, what do you see? Let's learn from those bold enough to believe. May we, too, gain the courage to illuminate the beauty that lives inside.

Today I'm highlighting my inspiration.

"Parietal Artist" Gabbie!

Cupcake

Eat the cupcake, yea, go ahead! Just for today, enjoy! Leave the dishes alone, turn off the news maybe even silence your phone. Take time for the one who takes care of everyone else. So why would I ask someone to spiral into dietary decadence and shrug tending to daily chores? When the pressure of expectations is paused, it allows for refocusing and relieves tunnel vision. It allows us to look around and see what else is there. We can then see what is up close and far away, not just through the peripheral view of our duties. We can see what we are missing.

It's your life and our planet; experience it as fully as possible. Yes, I'm suggesting clarity, readjusting, and reprioritizing through reading a book, going barefoot, or lying out in the sun; just be you. See and feel, breathe in what's going on around you today. Immerse yourself in you, that person who has been screaming to become a higher priority. There is a certain relief or grounding found in not being your own afterthought.

Find time today to view the world through the lens of a cupcake! The world's problems will still be there tomorrow, I promise, then decide which ones to pick back up. Your needs are also important; when met, it's then we can better serve.

Harold and Bonnie Sachs

Maters

There is a "Mater" sandwich in my future or possibly a BLT. I have other plants that have been productive, but something has been eating them first. Then I got to thinking I can't really blame the bird, bug, or little critter that is partaking in the same thing I want, they like tomatoes too!

Perhaps sharing is more important than just obtaining, gotta be a deeper context in there somewhere but for now I just want to enjoy the view and the anticipation of what is to come!

Back to School

I found this cube or block of wood on my desk. I don't know where it came from, but it has five words printed on it that tell me someone has me clocked pretty well. I smile when I look at it.

Last night it was bedtime for my Granddaughters, and Grandma began rounding them up, amongst complaints of I'm not tired, and Grandpa doesn't have to go to bed. I smile as they walk by and make comments about how right now would be a great time to watch some funny cat videos! Grandma conceded I was soon piled up; I think she loves hearing the boisterous laughter, even if it keeps her up a little longer.

But even Grandpas have their limits, and after several episodes of "cat fails," I, too, was ready to retire for the evening. Now I recognize bedtime stall techniques, but as we were getting ready, my 8-year-old expressed a real concern. The school would be starting back in just two weeks. And she's going into the 4th grade. She wanted to know what grades were difficult for me and other things we don't normally discuss, like what was the name of my favorite pet growing up. It reminded me of a little boy who, over a half-century ago, made a similar inquiry to his predecessor. Those conversations I, too, have tried to capture those in these writings. We talked about everything and nothing, and I could sense her calming down and relaxing. Worries seem to be darker at night when we are tired, and I didn't shrug off these concerns. For someone in single digits, they are just as traumatic as our major events.

I thought about it for a while last night and again this evening. Being there for someone, not necessarily with all the answers or solutions, but our presence when someone has a need is sometimes more important than words. As she left to go upstairs, she applied reciprocity and brought one of her stuffed kitties to my bedside to comfort me.

Kindness can be listening, which in and of itself is an action.

It says in this moment of your life, you are not alone!

Hearts Design

If you are unique in the life of a creative person, be it a writer, musician, sculptor, or artist, you live inside them close to the heart. That influence and those feelings are also reflected in their works. It's there, interwoven; it's a tapestry or mosaic attempting to capture, tell, or replicate the vision they have of you.

It's a form of immortality; your essence that triggered the inspiration is put into tangible form and stored... so that the time you had together can be revisited. This expression created is a physical representation of the invisible. It's the part of you that lives inside them, born from a combination of memory, imagination, and intimacy.

It's my guess you are in many stories and much artwork, in between the lines, in the curve of the marble, and in every resonant note.

Uplifting

Why are you smiling, my wife inquired as she peered over her coffee cup. She had observed me glancing and then reacting to the occupants of one of 3 fancy elevators at the hotel where we stayed last Friday. The glass walls were facing inwards to the open atrium. From my vantage point, where we were enjoying a late breakfast, I watched a young family with suitcases in tow on their vertical journey up to their room.

The youngest of the two boys carefully edged over to the transparent wall, and during the ascent, I read a resounding, almost audible wow from his pursed lips that was quickly replaced with a smile. I believe a child's sense of wonder and excitement is contagious, and by my wife reading my expression, I can say it's confirmed.

We were not traveling the same path, even going in the same direction. And these little ones' time will be a different one, but I'm not concerned. We who have journeyed all these years need to share values and traditions but also affirm the belief that we can walk a different way. They may find a trail we couldn't see, and when it's their moment to step out and share with the world, they will do it better. We are sending what is best of us forward. They are the results of many generations and thousands of loves.

Our species is going to be okay as long as they have that sense of purpose and retain that childhood wonder. They will adapt and work to resolve not only the issues we couldn't but ones that haven't been invented or yet exist.

These are the "good ole days" of our youth. Let's advise, guide, and contribute, and when it's time, let's get out of the way of the now little ones on their way up to future history.

Desolate

Dunes of granite rock formed the beach along the shoreline. There is little soil here and no trees. The buildings these structures are stout in appearance; they are built almost as if they were leaning, bracing for the Greenland winter winds that are soon to come. I took time to ponder the stillness. Except for the inland breeze, it's quiet, and I could only imagine the solitude of the senses after the blanketing snow arrived. The scalloped clouds, way above, move almost indiscernibly. They are taking their time moving across the blue and fluid to the harsh and desolate. A man could be tested here in more than one way.

One structure caught my eye. An A-frame building with an unusual dormer stood out in design and height. A brisk stroll satisfied my curiosity; it was indeed a church in this small village of Nanortalik. As I approached the entrance, a lady exiting said you can really feel it in there, and I found her observation to be true. I stopped short of the lectern or pulpit and just gathered my thoughts. Even with the door open, this is a warm place to be. After my prayer, I spoke to a lady seated at the rear of the church, an Inuit elder. A smile is universal. I commented and made a gesture that their church was beautiful. She got the message and nodded appreciatively.

About halfway back, three generations of the same family were selling their wares. One of the members was a business-minded 5- or 6-year-old girl. She was selling drawings, about a dozen and a half or so, of cats, and my eyes were fixed on the in the corner, a pink one at that! I gestured to the one I wanted to purchase, and she removed the four granite pebbles that secured each work of art to the makeshift table lying on the ground. One dollar, please she said in her tiny voice, prompted by her mom.

I then tried to share with this young girl, that I would sharing the drawing with my granddaughter, who also likes to draw cats. I told her mother that I was an author and her drawing would be in my next book. Her reaction showed she understood more English than I thought, and she related it in her native tongue to the others. I'm not sure who made whose day, but we were all happy in that moment of time that meant much but passed so quickly.

As we walked away, I shared with my wife I wish I would have taken a picture of her holding the drawing. She agreed and went back and asked permission to take the photo and shared a fee for allowing us to capture the moment for you, the readers.

The picture and her drawing will soon be on

my wall in my office, a moment in time, a touching of cultures and ages.

We are at sea now as I write this, headed to Canada, then back to New York. We are going to be okay people no matter what century it is or where we go, as long as we have hope as long as we have God and our children. In my experience, we wish for the same things.

Equation

Love cannot be measured. Poets site How do I love thee, let me count the ways. They may use things of great magnitude to form analogies, higher than any mountain or deeper than any ocean. It warms the heart to believe in something that's greater than self and what can be envisioned. It's so important that people will give their most precious resource, their time, and their lives to obtain and defend it. Many have said things like I will love you forever x infinity to describe not only in width, height, and breath but effectively adding times dimension to the equation.

So, I don't believe it can be measured, but even the most stoic or skeptic cannot deny its existence. I do believe it can be described by something Einstein called "spooky action at a distance," better known as quantum entanglement. Two particles, once joined and separated by enormous distances, instantly react to what happens to the other, even on opposite sides of the known universe. There is something that touches each of us that binds us, and affects us all; we are connected, and that conduit is God, and God is love.

Morning

The critters are beginning to scurry about as I, too, greet the dawn. The blanket of dew will soon be pulled back as the sun climbs higher, and the rest of the world will soon awaken. It's quiet but not the absence of sound; it's the absence of noise; life is all around me. As I type, a Woodpecker sends out Morse code echoing through the valley in these hills of Tennessee. Other than my side glance, I become motionless as I admire a visitor who lands next to me on the front porch railing. Our moment is fleeting, and then it's off to continue his search for breakfast.

Ahh, the sun peaked over the hills, trees, and fine mist that separates us. With my coffee and its touch, I'm now warm as I had questioned being out barefoot in this first cool morning of autumn.

You know, I've found those who have been cold have a greater appreciation for the warmth; those who have suffered what seemed an eternal night crave the light.

Find comfort in the dawn; these are the moments, and this is your day.

Good morning, fellow travelers! Thanks for sharing a moment in my journey!

Stones River

This past Saturday, we met to drop off our Grandchildren. Halfway is Murfreesboro, TN, and my Son suggested we meet at Stones River National Park. The timing couldn't have been better, as we were treated to a concert and a narration providing the history of the songs they performed. To my immediate right was a reenactment camp where some men had gathered and would later fire the five cannons. The soldiers and many of the musicians were in period dress, so it gave the performance a further sense of authenticity. Just beyond the camp were the white tombstones of the soldiers who died that early day in January long ago. Like Arlington, it was hauntingly quiet. The last song they performed was Home Sweet Home. The narrator explained that the bands and voices from each army would attempt to overpower each other in the evening. But as they played this one melancholy melody, the musicians from the regiments on both sides of the river joined together. She went on to comment that if there hadn't been a river between them, the war might have ended that night.

I found deep-reaching poetry in her words that early evening because no one wants peace more than a soldier.

Turf Wars

I am sitting out front this morning with coffee in hand like I do most days. The five crows haven't shown up yet, but it seems an additional squirrel has taken residency in our corner of the neighborhood. Guess I'll start naming them soon; old men do that. The maple tree across the road is displaying its brilliant colors; I anticipate it each year. The hues are gently cascading down the branches from red to green, but it will be the first to shed its modesty as the leaves at the apex have already begun their journey back to the earth. Time and the seasons change more than just the landscape. We as well adapt as we must to remain viable. So, I've stopped admiring the conifers, deciduous trees, birds, and furry critters that inhabit them; I am enjoying a moment of appreciation. I'm glancing over the terrain I carefully mow and edge. There are bicycle tracks, torn turf, and spots where my grandchildren wrestled each other to the ground. It's a beautiful site, a testament to the memories created there just days ago.

Speed and strength give way to time, but nature also rewards the years. We slow down; that's not a choice, but with that comes an appreciation and enjoyment of all that is happening around us. We aren't missing out on life because we aren't as ambulatory or agile. We are no longer hurried; we enjoy it more because we live in the moments and create memories. Time, we can't slow it, but we can capture it.

P

Peppers

Yesterday, I planted six persimmon seeds and 12 walnuts from my son's farm in Tennessee. I have them divided into large pots filled with some soil I purchased from the local nursery. I got a small fig tree on sale recently, but I have delayed planting it. This morning, I gave it a permanent home in the red clay soil of Alabama. The mums I bought my wife for decorating needs some water, so in a few, I'll go out front and give them a drink. I took time to find the "hedge clippers" kind of heavy-duty scissors. I found them out back as my grandchildren helped Grandpa this past weekend by trimming the hedges near the fence. I need these to harvest some Habaneros and Chili Peppers. Like the tomatoes we have in abundance, we typically give a lot away, but I'm keeping a few and drying them. My mother used to do that, and even in their dehydrated state, hanging on a string, they are still a beautiful red.

So why the reflective state as we move from summer to fall? There is a lot of stuff going on in the world, but somehow, this morning, I had a calming sense of peace. As I watered the cherry trees, I had planted this past spring, a quote came to me from a book I read.

1 To everything there is a season and a time to every purpose under the heaven:

2 A time to be born, and a time to die; a time to plant, and a time to pluck up that which is planted.

3 A time to kill and a time to heal; a time to break down and a time to build up.

4 A time to weep, and a time to laugh; a time to mourn, and a time to dance.

5 A time to cast away stones, and a time to gather stones together; a time to embrace, and a time to refrain from embracing.

6 A time to get and a time to lose; a time to keep, and a time to cast away.

7 A time to rend, and a time to sew; a time to keep silence, and a time to speak;8 A time to love and a time to hate; a time of war and a time of peace.

Life is a dynamic state of change. We must plan, adapt, and enjoy the fruits of our labor—everything in its due time.

Gifts

If you are born with a God-given talent, developed and refined over time, it can do more than make us pause and marvel; it can take our breath away! That uniqueness can become a catalyst or perhaps a beacon to others. It can provide clarity from what was once shadowed and, above all else, hope.

It's also a statement of self, for each work is a reflection of the artist, architect, or engineer. Not only the vision and concepts but also the personality and beliefs are poured into the author's work to take form in the thoughts of the admirer.

Shapes are generated, and other worlds are created, visited, or explained; ah, this curiosity thing, it always evolves and yields to wonder. That view or path you create is a window to a world, yet unnoticed, it's an appreciation or explanation for what was there all the time. This comes with the removal of the shroud, a revealing of what is, what will be, and what is possible.

Though they are yours, don't take them with you when you leave. Let them grow; let them come to fruition in the hearts and minds of those who travel with you and those who are to follow.

Share that we may all benefit. Let the

world, let the heavens know you were here!

THERE WILL BE A DAY
WHEN YOU CAN
NO LONGER DO THIS
THAT DAY IS
NOT TODAY

Soup and Ice-cream

I mean, I like Ribeye as much as anyone, but there is something about soup, especially in the fall, that I enjoy. Mother used to say it would "hold you up" or "stick to your ribs," and I agree armed with a big bowl, a glass of milk, and a PBJ, there's not a whole lot in your day you can't tackle.

If you spend some time in Arlington or Dallas, expect it to be chili. New Orleans has more flavor in their gumbo than should be allowed, and if you visit New England, their Clam Chowder is delicious!

I can say in our palate, we can be divided in what is best or what we enjoy, but we are actually different in other ways as well. Sunday morning, we can choose to go to different houses of worship, but on Sunday afternoon, be united in the Jersey we wear supporting our mutual Team.

We can choose to listen or play music; either way, we can sway, move, or clap to the rhythm. It has a way of uniting us second only to ice cream! And there are those out there I envy... the lyrists that immortalize an emotion and help see the event they are describing so well we feel it too. A melody mixed copiously with gifted words that touch body and soul. These things aren't localized but universal.

There are those who disagree, but if given a heartfelt listen, we can at least understand where they are coming from and we can also learn from it. If our opinions still differ, it only reinforces our own beliefs, but if we are corrected, growth occurs. This type of communication, at the least, validates both participants. Most of them want to know they've been heard and understood. There will always be differences! There are those who love the noise and the wind from the fan when they sleep and those who don't! Chances are they are married!

Shouting or chanting is seldom conducive to communication; it's counter-intuitive, but the louder the volume, the more it's squelched by the ears. Instead, plant a seed of peace; nothing raises self-esteem like being heard, actually being listened to (pausing before reply is classy).

Every wise teacher will learn from their students. Since we already know all we know, listening or reading prompts and stimulates new growth. It's as simple as I can figure it out or learn from the mind of another.

If we look closely enough, there are plenty of things we can agree on out there. (except for the belief butter pecan is better than black walnut, then we are going to have issues.) However, like the differences in our food, we can enjoy the spices and flavors. What I am suggesting is that we acknowledge the same and enjoy the differences. We are more alike than not!

(P.S.Breyers is best)

When you know you've married a great woman!

The internet is a great place to argue with total strangers about religion, politics, and, well, pretty much any and everything! But I may have found an exception! Few women will argue with the fact that their husbands can't find anything in the house. Ann will ask me why I opened another jar of strawberry jelly. My reply was "that there was not any in the fridge". She opens the door and points to the two other jars I've opened previously that somehow appear in plain view. It used to scare me, but I just accept it now!! It's almost like she can complete my sentences...have you seen my...? Yes, you left it on the nightstand. This goes for belts, my Bible, and the number one most asked question by men are... (in my best Richard Dawson voice) Where are my car keys?

Well, it is cool that she is and has always been there for me, and that alone is a solid reason for saying she's the one, but this morning, she gave me yet another!

I have been missing my key FOB to her expedition for about two weeks. Since it didn't appear out of thin air, I felt I should go look for it. So, Ann saw me running around with my DeWalt flashlight and inquired about my obvious search. Still willing to blame it on car key gnomes, I told her I was going to go look for it inside her vehicle. Well, she went around the other way, and we met each other at the entrance that goes out to the garage. We paused at this mutual impasse. I didn't budge either, but I noticed she slowly raised and tightened her grip on her flashlight. She stared at me patiently and deliberately...waiting. I pointed my light upwards, making my best lightsaber noise, and she never blinked, clicked hers on, accepted the challenge, and it was on. You got to keep it fun, folks!!

Today's pics are of our futuristic weapons; they also serve as flashlights and are centered to show off her decorating in the Formal Dining!

I did find the FOB (all by myself)

Double O 64

It becomes apparent as you get older that you can't do some of the things you used to enjoy as well or at all. Yeah, that's smart! Anyway, each of us has a way of dealing with this issue as the decades begin to add up, and I thought I would share mine. I became a secret agent. 007 was taken, and since I'm older, I've selected 0064, and here is my latest covert, stealth, mission.

It was just a routine job, but those are the easiest to let your guard down, so while relaxed, I was at the ready! I loaded my assignment (leftover chili) into the magnetron chamber (microwave). The task was simple, and the timer was set. I pressed the start button and sighed. There was no turning back now the countdown had begun. About halfway through my mission, I heard footsteps from above; it was just the wind; I comforted myself, but then it got louder till I heard the pronounced click of her shoes coming down the stairs. Take deep breaths, I said to myself, and remember your training; still, I could feel the intensity building as my respiration and HR increased. The clock somehow clicked slower. I've got this, but I had to decide to abort or to continue on and play it cool. I choose the latter. She entered the room, and she seemed to know something was amiss, but to her credit, she stayed calm, voice not wavering as she approached me. The timer was still counting down, just a few moments left, and with my task completed, I could scurry away with my prize to the relative safety of my Headquarters (office). She walked past, and I let out an audible sigh and then froze; she asked the question we both knew the answer to, and she was waiting to see how I responded.

In my sense of adventure, I had not put that small plate over the chili to prevent the beans from exploding like small grenades all over the internal structure of this microwave generator. I had forgotten the illumination feature of this device that allows others to see the content. I had miss-timed her pace and distance as well as her resolve. I quickly acquired the device required to retain the heated protein energy of the chili beans and "made safe" the chamber.

This victory belongs to her, but tomorrow is another day! Later this week, clandestine mattress tag removal, running with scissors and socks not in but near the hamper!!

Fred and Ginger

During our morning coffee, my wife pointed and exclaimed look over there. I glanced upward in time to see the results of a stiff breeze in our neighbor's trees. Hundreds of bright-colored leaves were pirouetting downward to form a patchwork quilt on the ground. They had almost reached their destination when a crosswind caught them back up and sent them scurrying across the street with a skip. I could hear the applause of the remaining foliage, and the clapping of the dried leaves stirred by the same wind while they patiently waited for their chance to perform.

Ginger and Fred would be amazed. These unchoreographed leaps and lifts rival the human variant of motion and connection. Synchronized and rhythmic, a figure skater or the best of our ballet would yield to this annual performance.

What a moment, Mother Nature conducting a private showing of her ballroom dancing.

Less is more, sometimes!

It's a term you've heard before less is more, and it has many applications, not excluding cologne and perfume. It's seen in one of my favorite quotes from David Thoreau: Simplify, Simplify, Simplify. So, a minimalist approach can be desired and, with that, a less cluttered and perhaps aromatic life. This train of thought can even be extended to art and writing. In a painting or an article, there is a time when it is finished. No more birds or adjectives, trees, or haystacks; the work is complete.

That's the challenge; there must be enough substance to have meaning, to get the message, experience, or thought across. But the benefits of brevity must be compared to what would make it verbose. Is it necessary to convey the thought? Does it add or take away in its presentation? But be mindful that what may be considered eccentric may be there for a reason. Authors, artists, and songwriters include minutia that is esoteric, yes, just for a few, or perhaps it's a personal "note" that only they will understand. It speaks to the masses, but the deeper parts are only heard by a few; this private echo of words or craft. It's a fingerprint and a treasure hidden in the prose and canvas. The artisan gives an external view, and if you are meticulous and patient enough, an internal one is there as well.

An author has an idea that excites an emotion, his desire; the goal is to pen with clarity. "I could see and feel what you wrote" is the most desired accolades. Writing is transference! It's magic that it's excluded from the boundaries of time. The thoughts, the essence, this part will remain.

So, pick up the pen and paint with words!

Say What?

Earlier this week, we picked up our grandkids at school. On the way back, we were jamming to the oldies on the radio when a song from CCR began to play. The song Bad Moon Rising has been out for half a century and still has one of the most understood lyrics! Well, when it came time I let loose on the misheard lyric, they both began giggling. So, when that lyric and tagline came around again, we all belted it out loud and then busted out laughing!

If you look in the Book of Grandpas that is handed down through the years, in chapter 17, second paragraph on page 397, it says, "Grandpa must be willing to have fun with, said Grandchildren at any time, including but not limited to mischief or fun they may not know about yet." I felt this moment loosely qualified and used it as a teaching moment. I introduced them to songs like:

Pat Benatar - Hit me with your pet shark!

Eddie Money _ I've got two chickens in parrot ties!

Starship - We built this city on sausage rolls!

Yes, we help them grow and add a little fun along the way, but we too benefit. They keep us young!

Beyond Silence

If you are learning to play an instrument almost immediately, you begin hearing songs in a different way. The notes, the melody, and the chorus were there all these decades, but learning their intricacies makes you wonder what else have I missed in all these years of passive listening. What was there all the time when I didn't know how to listen?

We don't have to understand why the harmonies sound good to enjoy them, but it is fun to explore! It's like looking into the eyes of a lover; the words may entice, but such things that move and drive humans go much further, deeper in the soul.

For that, you should find a rare individual, those who can seem to dance without music, and teach us how to hear.

Superman

I enjoy getting up early, just before dawn, and obtaining that first cup of the elixir of life! The house is quiet, and in my freshly awakened state, in my view, the world, too, is still resting. I've learned the joy of reading as the rays begin to reach through the windows. I'm different now. I study till I come to the point where I need to digest what the author is saying. I then ponder it to see how it applies to me. It's no longer a type or need of a competition of completion but a yearning for understanding! This morning, it was the Good Book. I read only one chapter and then put it down. Mulling over the author's offerings, I began to think about some of the challenges we face on this planet. And this is what I've decided, at least for the day...I'm not going to solve the world's problems; I'm going to work on myself and this shell in which I live.

It's in the stillness and serenity of this stage of my life that I find my peace. I search for what I need to address more so than the shortcomings or differences of others. I have plenty to work on right here, but if you see me running around in a cape tomorrow, you'll know I found a different inspiration. You have to be careful what you read first thing in the morning!

Veterans Day

This Saturday is Veterans Day; please take the time to thank all the Veterans from each generation. But this year, also take a moment and thank the spouses and families. The spouse has to be both Mom and Dad, covering all the bases during the absences, and many first words and steps are missed by those serving!

There is a part of a Veteran that doesn't come back; it remains there far away but visits the dreams of soldiers and sailors alike. It's for a lifetime. It doesn't go away. We are grateful and do appreciate the recognition of the sacrifice. But if a Veteran doesn't respond well, perhaps he shares a common belief that the accolades should be for those who got busted up worse than we did or didn't make it back...those who paid a greater price for the freedoms we often take for granted. Understand nobody comes back the same...and when you do come home, the families can see it in the eyes and mannerisms you've changed. So part is taken from the family as well, so remember, thank them.

With Gratitude and Respect

To the Grunts, Zoomies, Squids, and Ground Pounders and those who patiently waited, I salute you

USS Forrestal CV59

Gifted

Gerald Alvis

The Poet of Greenlawn

We've all known that person, the one who gets straight A's in math but didn't study or take a book home. There are those who pick up music quickly and play so that we can enjoy them harmonizing with others or just singing with their instrument.

Someone can be knowledgeable, intelligent, or witty; it could be said a person is wise or has wisdom. Indeed, the words could be considered synonyms, but it's like memorization, theory, and application; they go together but also can be different skill sets.

But in my experience, one talent is even more desirable, and its effect goes far behind the individual expressing the gift.

Some can see the glimmer of light in the eyes of another human being. They can encourage and empower those with fledgling beliefs and skills. They can see the ability and potential in others and are a catalyst… and that's all it takes sometimes. And to me, recognizing and giving to that cause is real genius.

Shapes

Herringbone and washboard each could be used to describe the clouds I viewed today. Some were interlaced with the trails of travelers streaking across the sky. The patterns are symmetrical, and I wonder about the external forces and wind currents that shape them. It's almost like they were created for us, shaped, and then put on display for us to admire, and I do as they scroll past.

If you're a scuba diver, something similar can be seen in the sand. As the waves rock back and forth toward the shore, they create patterns not unlike their heavenly counterparts. A diver can use these to tell when they are getting near the beach as the ridges and indentions of these displays become closer.

The dunes of the desert are scalloped with such, as each speck of sand awaits its turn in line to crest and then leap from its peaks.

But we are different. There is no doubt that we are affected by external forces, but we humans, more so, are shaped by what moves us inside, and that's for us to decide.

ALABAMA

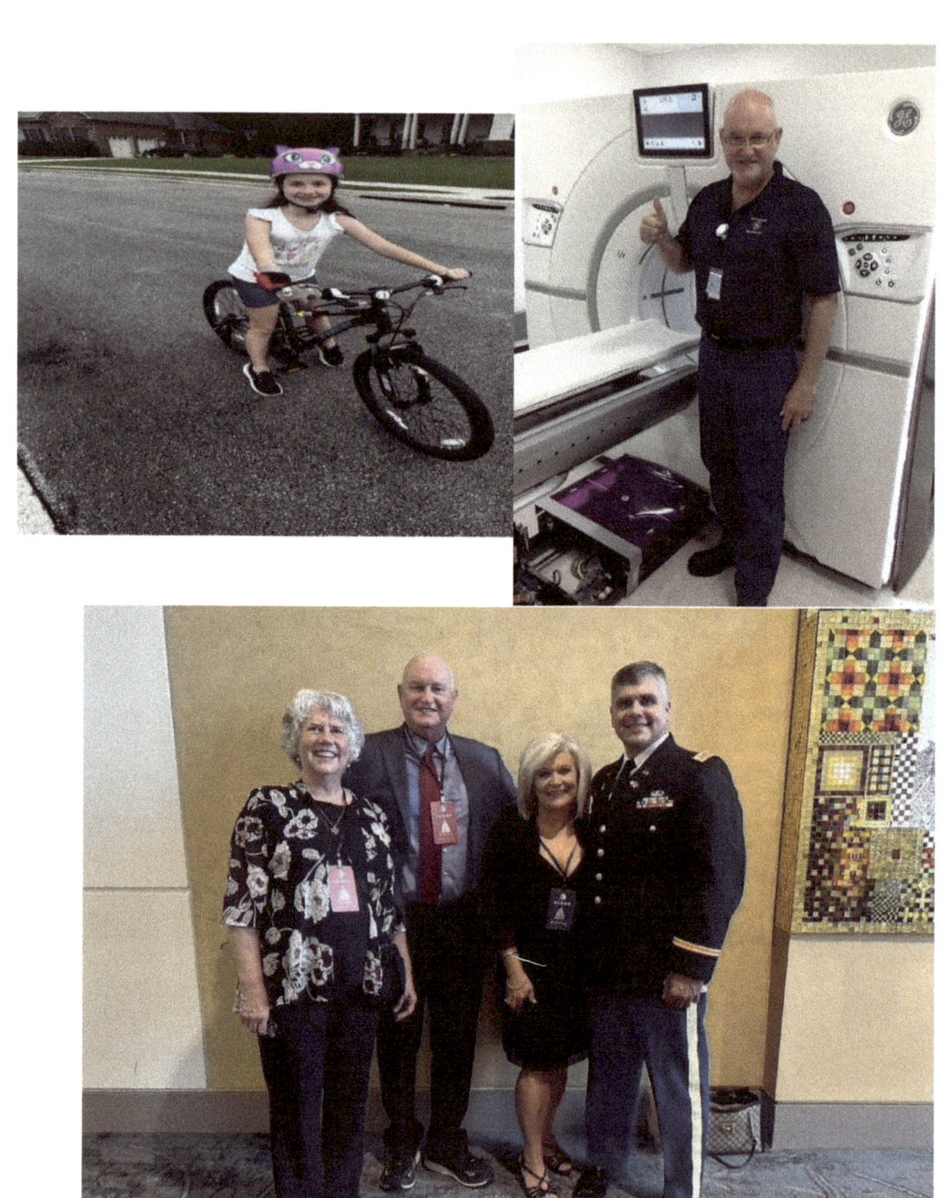

Mahogany Bay

JACK DANIELS
Old No. 7
Tennessee
WHISKEY

Larry Veahman
A gifted and athlete and man!
Here's to many adventures and many more!

Zack and the Katester Holt

Krista, Alea and Jud Baldwin

Drew and Jake Baldwin

M Baldwin

Hanging out with a Stateman!

Harold Sachs
In Memory

Steve and Leah
Nora Abigail and Emma Patti

Nancy Veahman and Her Awesome Brother!

To my Viking Sister with Love!

3 Sisters

And in memory of:

 Toppy, Luella, Doris, Regina and Jack

Bryan and Chris

Kona

Thanks for watching over our Grandchildren and keeping us safe from Squirrels, the light monster, and budgers!

Thanks for being the neighborhood pet.

Here is to

"Fair winds and following seas!"

and

"Ancient evenings and distant music".

www.ingramcontent.com/pod-product-compliance
Lightning Source LLC
Chambersburg PA
CBHW041202150726
48006CB00016B/2076